CONTENTS

Did you hear about the mad scientist who invented a gas that could burn through anything? Now he's trying to invent something to hold it in!

What do you do with a dead science teacher? Barium.

What do you call it when you get struck by lightning? A shocking experience.

Why did the science teacher tell the student he should become a weather reporter? Because he was an expert on wind.

REALLY HORRIBLE JOKES

REALLY HORRIBLE SCIENCE JOKES

KAREN KING AND PATIENCE COSTER

W
FRANKLIN WATTS
LONDON•SYDNEY

First published in 2014 by Franklin Watts

Copyright © 2014 Arcturus Publishing Limited

Franklin Watts
338 Euston Road
London NW1 3BH

Franklin Watts Australia
Level 17/207 Kent Street, Sydney NSW 2000

Produced by Arcturus Publishing Limited,
26/27 Bickels Yard, 151–153 Bermondsey Street, London SE1 3HA

Editors: Patience Coster and Joe Harris
All images: Shutterstock
Layout designer: Elaine Wilkinson
Cover designers: Elaine Wilkinson and Trudi Webb

A CIP catalogue record for this book is available from the British Library.
Dewey Decimal Classification Number 818.6'02
ISBN 978 1 4451 3150 4
Printed in China

Franklin Watts is a division of Hachette Children's Books,
an Hachette UK company.
www.hachette.co.uk

SL003843EN
Supplier 03, Date 1113, Print Run 3067

Mouse 1: I've trained that crazy scientist at last!

Mouse 2: How have you done that?

Mouse 1: I'm not sure, but every time I run through the maze and ring the bell, he gives me a lump of cheese.

How do you tell the difference between the sciences?
If it stinks, it's chemistry; if it's green or wriggly, it's biology; and if it doesn't work, it's physics.

What were the scientist's last words?
Now for the taste test.

Did you hear about the mad scientist who put dynamite in his fridge?
They say he blew his cool.

How many drops of acid does it take to make a stink bomb?
Quite a phew.

What sort of ghosts haunt chemistry labs?
Methylated spirits.

How do you make antifreeze?
Steal her pyjamas.

How can you tell that your chemistry teacher has died?
He fails to react.

Susan: My science teacher reminds me of the sea.
Dad: Really, dear. Do you mean she's deep and calm, but sometimes stormy?
Susan: No, she makes me sick!

What sign did the science teacher hang on the lab door?
Gone nuclear fission.

If a lightning bolt hits the back of a train, how long will it take to reach the driver?
It depends on whether he's a good conductor.

My teacher threw sodium chloride at me.
That's a salt!

What's the most important thing to remember in chemistry?
Don't lick the spoon.

Two atoms bumped into each other.
First atom: Oh dear, I think I've lost an electron!
Second atom: Are you sure?
First atom: I'm positive!

What's special about irradiated cats?
They have 18 half-lives.

What did one lightning bolt say to the other lightning bolt?
You're shocking.

What do you call robot poo?
R2 doo doo.

Astronomy teacher: Now, who can tell me what kind of star is dangerous? **Student: A shooting star!**

What do clones wear? Designer genes.

What do constipated mathematicians do? Work it out with a pencil.

What should you do if you swallow a light bulb? Spit it out and be delighted.

A mosquito was heard
to complain
That a chemist had
poisoned his brain.
The cause of his sorrow
Was paradichloro-
diphenyltrichloroethane.

Why did the
chemist cut off
one of her legs?
To reduce her
carbon footprint.

Teacher:
Can you tell
me what HNO_3 is?
Student: Um . . . It's on
the tip of my tongue, sir.
Teacher: Well, you'd
better spit it out, it's
nitric acid!

What's a maths teacher's favourite type of toilet paper?
Multi-ply.

Teacher: You remind me of the planet Jupiter.
Student: Why is that?
Teacher: You're dense and gassy.

Why did the chemistry teacher tell so many bad jokes?
Because all the good ones argon.

Seen on the door to a lightwave lab: Do not look into laser with remaining good eye.

Why do chemists call helium, curium and barium the medical elements? Because if you can't helium or curium, you barium!

What do you call a king's fart? A noble gas.

Why did Pete change his name to Coal?
He was under pressure.

Where does illegal light end up?
In a prism.

A priest, a lawyer and an engineer are to be guillotined. The priest puts his head on the block, the rope is pulled, and nothing happens. He declares he's been saved by divine intervention and is released. The lawyer puts his head on the block, and again, the rope doesn't release the blade. He claims he can't be executed twice for the same crime and is set free. The engineer places his head under the guillotine. He looks up at the release mechanism and says: "Wait a minute, I see your problem . . ."

DISGUSTING DISEASES JOKES

What is a computer virus?
A terminal illness.

Doctor: I have some good news.
Patient: What is it?
Doctor: We are going to name a disease after you.

Why did the germ cross the microscope?
To get to the other slide.

How do you make a tissue dance?
Put a little boogie in it.

What's green and hangs off trees?
Giraffe snot.

What's a sick joke?
Something that comes up in conversation.

Surgeon: I'm afraid we have to operate on you again. You see, I left my rubber gloves inside you.
Patient: I don't mind paying for them, if you'll just leave me alone.

Scientists say that 90% of all £5 notes carry germs.
Not true! Even a germ can't live on a fiver these days.

Why did the computer keep sneezing?
It had a virus.

Why did the cookie go to the hospital?
Because he felt crumb-y.

Have you seen the movie Constipated?
No, it hasn't come out yet.

Doctor, Doctor, I think I'm a bridge!
What's come over you?
Two cars, a truck and a bus.

Where do you bury lopsided people?
A-symmetry.

Patient: Doctor, you've taken out my tonsils, my adenoids, my gallbladder, my varicose veins and my appendix, but I still don't feel well.
Doctor: That's quite enough out of you!

How do crazy people go through the forest?
They take the psycho path.

Did you hear about the woman who went in for plastic surgery and came out looking like a Martian?
She told the surgeon she wanted to look like a million dollars, so he made her face all green and crinkly!

A chemist finds a man leaning against the wall of his shop. "What's wrong with him?" says the chemist. His assistant replies, "He came in for cough syrup, but I couldn't find any, so I gave him laxatives." "Idiot!" says the chemist. "You can't treat a cough with laxatives." "Of course you can," the assistant replies. "Look at him now, he's too afraid to cough!"

Patient: Doctor, you know those pills you gave me for my stomach?
Doctor: What about them?
Patient: They keep rolling off in the middle of the night!

Why did doctors abandon the custom of bloodletting? Because it was all in vein.

Why was the organ donor so tired after the operation?
He had really put his heart into it.

Deafness is becoming quite a problem for me. I never thought I'd hear myself say that.

Why should you never argue with your doctor?
Because he has inside information.

Why should you never lie to an X-ray technician? Because he can see right through you.

Why did the woman avoid funerals?
She was not a mourning person.

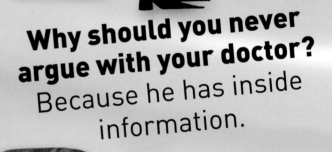

A man was recovering in the hospital after a serious accident. He shouted, "Doctor, doctor, I can't feel my legs!" The doctor replied, "I know, I've cut off your hands."

Doctor: That's a terrible cough you've got.
Patient: Consumption be done about it?

The medical student had to learn what the measles were. He did it from scratch.

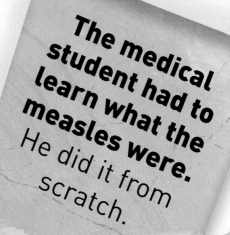

Without correct instruments, the surgeon had to operate using plumber's tools.
It was a gut-wrenching experience.

You say you have bad skin. I'd say that was a pore excuse.

Why should you be kind to your dentist? Because he has fillings, too.

Nurses who look after patients with spots do a great job. But sometimes they get paid a measley salary.

What happened to the skeleton that sat by the fire all night?
He was bone dry.

Why are fried onions like a photocopier?
They keep repeating themselves.

Why didn't the skeleton jump off the cliff?
Because he didn't have the guts.

Why did Frankenstein's monster have a stiff arm?
He had run out of elbow grease.

Why did the skeleton stay out in the snow all night?
He was a numbskull.

I don't think I should have eaten that chilli!
Why do you say that?
It's just a gut feeling.

What do you get when you cross a skunk with Frankenstein's monster?
Stinkenstein.

How do you make a skeleton laugh?
Tickle his funny bone.

How does Frankenstein's monster sit in his chair?
Bolt upright.

What kind of ship does Count Dracula sail in?
A blood vessel.

Did you know that you continue learning even when you are dead?
You can learn so much in your skull days!

Teacher: Can you name the three kinds of blood vessel?
Student: Yes. Arteries, veins and caterpillars.

If you're American when you're outside the bathroom, what are you when you are inside?
Eur-o-pean.

What's the funniest bone in the body?
The humerus.

I have to go to the doctor's, my neck's gone floppy!
Chin up!

I made a pot of fish eye soup.
It should see me through the week.

Professor: Today I will be talking about the liver and the spleen.
Student: Oh no, if there's one thing I can't stand, it's an organ recital!

What does Frankenstein's monster call a screwdriver?
Dad.

Which human organ never dies?
The liver!

What do you get if you cross a mouse and a deer?
Mickey Moose.

Dentist: I have to pull out your bad tooth, but don't worry, it will take just five minutes.
Patient: And how much will it cost?
Dentist: £90.00.
Patient: £90.00 for just a few minutes work???
Dentist: I can extract it very slowly if you like.

I crossed a phone with a skunk
And now the service stinks.

What do you get when you cross a potato with a sponge?
I don't know, but it sure holds a lot of gravy!

What did the man say when he found someone blocking his path to the toilet?
Urine my way.

Why are frogs so happy?
Because they can eat whatever bugs them.

What do you do when two snails have a fight?
Leave them to slug it out!

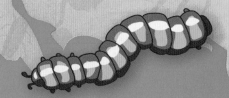

Where do bees go to the toilet?
At the BP station.

How can you tell which end of a worm is which?
Tickle it in the middle and see which end laughs.

There was an old woman from Ryde,
Who ate too many apples and died.
The apples fermented
Inside the lamented
And made cider inside her inside.

England doesn't have a kidney bank. But it does have a Liverpool.

Two silkworms had a race. They ended up in a tie.

I don't think I want a spine. It's holding me back.

First scientist: Did you know that I'm thinking of cloning myself? Second scientist: Now wouldn't that be just like you!

Glossary

adenoids A fleshy lump between the nose and the back of the throat.

astronomy The study of space.

barium A soft metal.

curium A radioactive metal.

electron Part of an atom.

fission The splitting of something into two or more parts. In physics, "fission" can mean nuclear fission, the splitting up of the centre of an atom.

methylated spirits A poisonous substance containing alcohol that can be used to dissolve things.

varicose veins Swollen and twisted veins.

Further Reading

King, Bart. *The Big Book of Gross Stuff*. Gibbs Smith, 2010.

Simon, Francesca. *Horrid Henry's Joke Book*. Orion Children's Books, 2004.

Stewart, Melissa. *Out of This World Jokes About the Solar System*. Enslow Elementary, 2012.

Websites

www.ducksters.com/jokesforkids/
A safe site with jokes on many categories, from history to sport, nature to some very silly jokes!

www.sciencekids.co.nz/jokes.html
Funny science-related jokes for kids.

Index